NEW CHARCOAL POWDER

SUPPLIES LIST _____3

CHARCOAL POWDER _____4

PROGRESSION PICTURE _____6

CREATING SHAPES_____8

PROGRESSING PICTURE_____ 10

SUPPLIES LIST

1. Charcoal powder
2. Vine charcoal soft
3. Charcoal Sache
4. Hard and Soft brick
5. Blender Stumps
6. Strathmore 400 series paper
7. Kneadederasers

Charcoal powder

The first thing to do is cover the paper in charcoal powder by using a sache bag. If you don't have sache bag you can use a soft napkin.

Using the round side of the bag or the napkin create the eye sockets and push values where needed: Darks/lights.

Note: You can use the vine charcoal to create powder and spread it across the paper with a napkin or sache bag

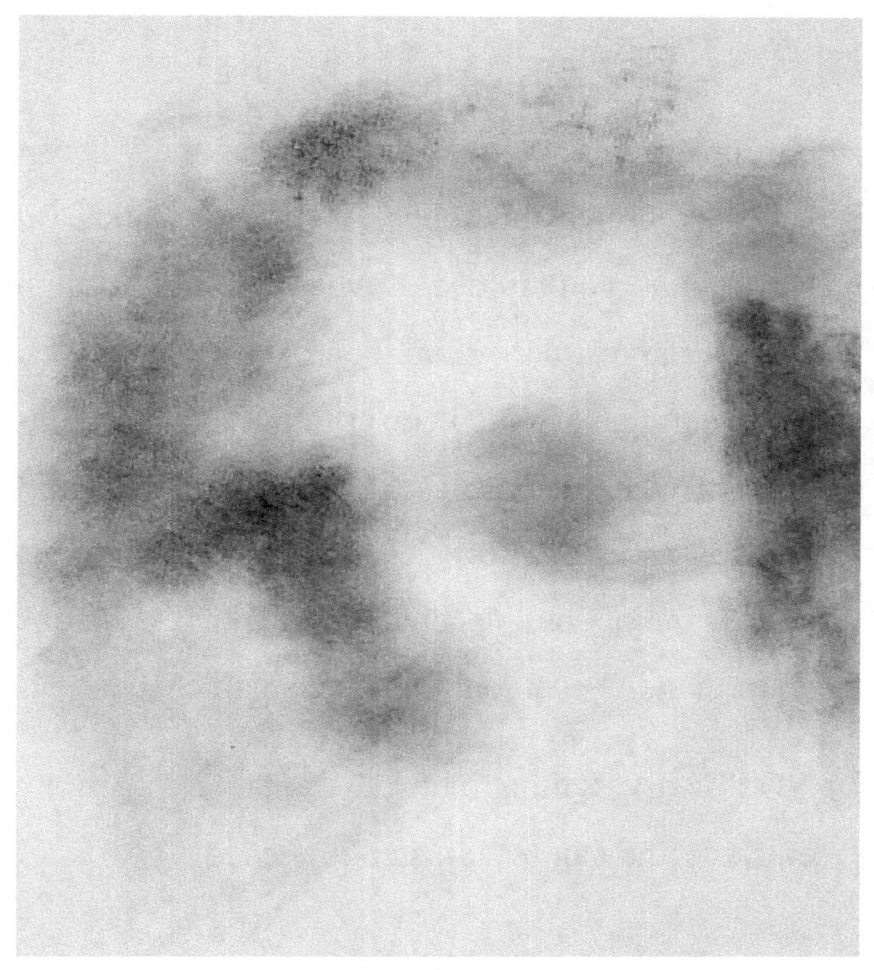

Progression Picture

portions are not as important here as the values are. Until we create the shapes in the next part. But it should give you an idea of where the lightest light is and the darkest dark should be. At this stage you can start using the kneaded eraser to put the highlights on the face where needed as we will see in the next part. As well as using the vine charcoal to create the eye shapes and overall placement of the face. By breaking apart the vine charcoal to create small shapes.

NOTE: Everything shown up until this point is erasable and can be adjusted if needed

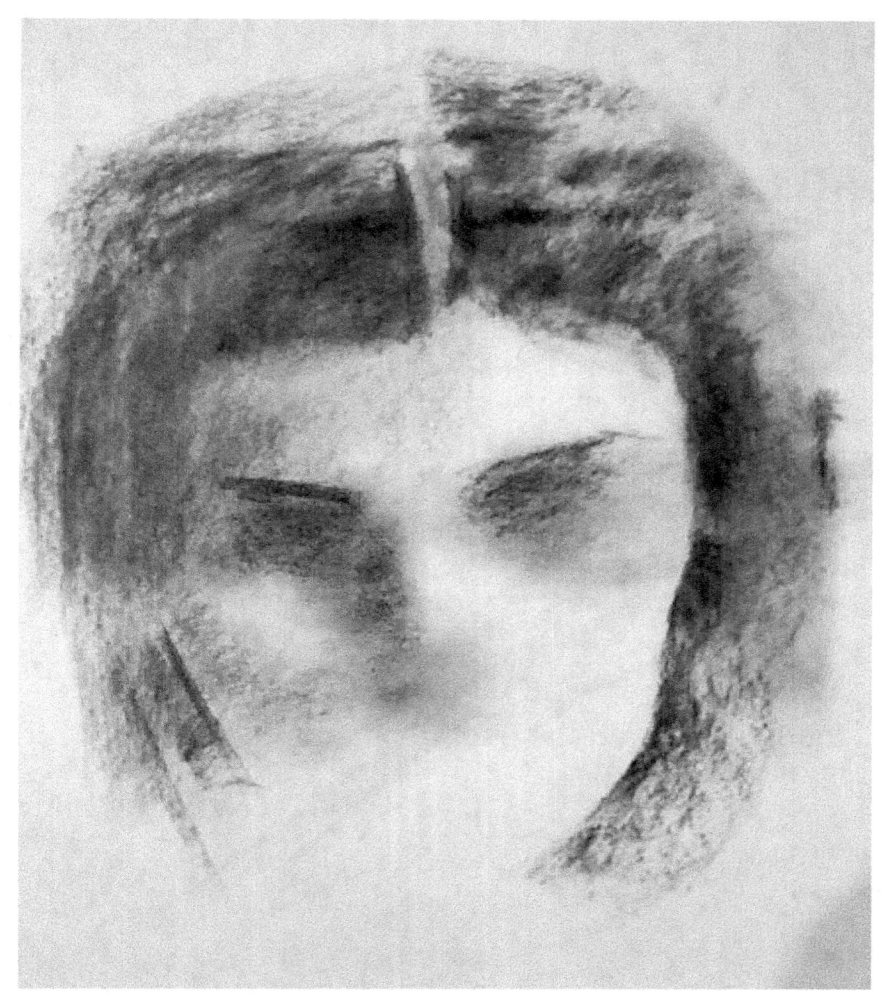

Creating Shapes

Tools used here are stumps, hard charcoal pencil and soft vine stick. By rolling the paper stump on the powder you can create the shapes needed to make the outline of the face as well as the placement of the eyes/eyebrows. At this point by using the stumps erasing to complete white is gonna be harder and less affective. So make sure your confident in the placement and go for it. Also using the vine to outline the face to build the overall shape.

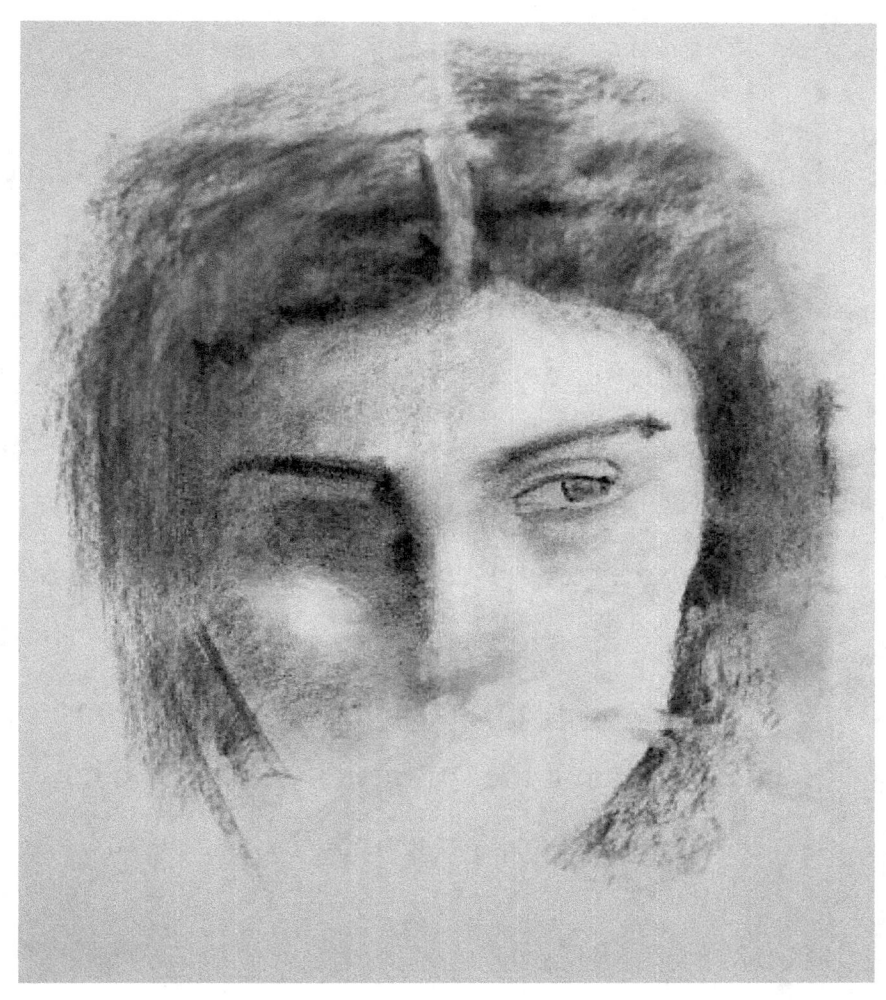

Progressing Picture

Don't think of the shadows as a drawing but as shapes, and you will soon see the illusion of a face. By using the vine to show value patterns can solidify the dark areas and then after, you can then come in with hard charcoal pencil to create the eyebrows and eye details. Remember that hard is first and then soft pencil is last of that specific area. Because the soft pencil will make everything pop while the hard pencil is more subtle. We want to sneak up on the drawing rather than trying to be perfect with the soft pencil. And if you mess up the soft pencil is less forgiving than the hard.

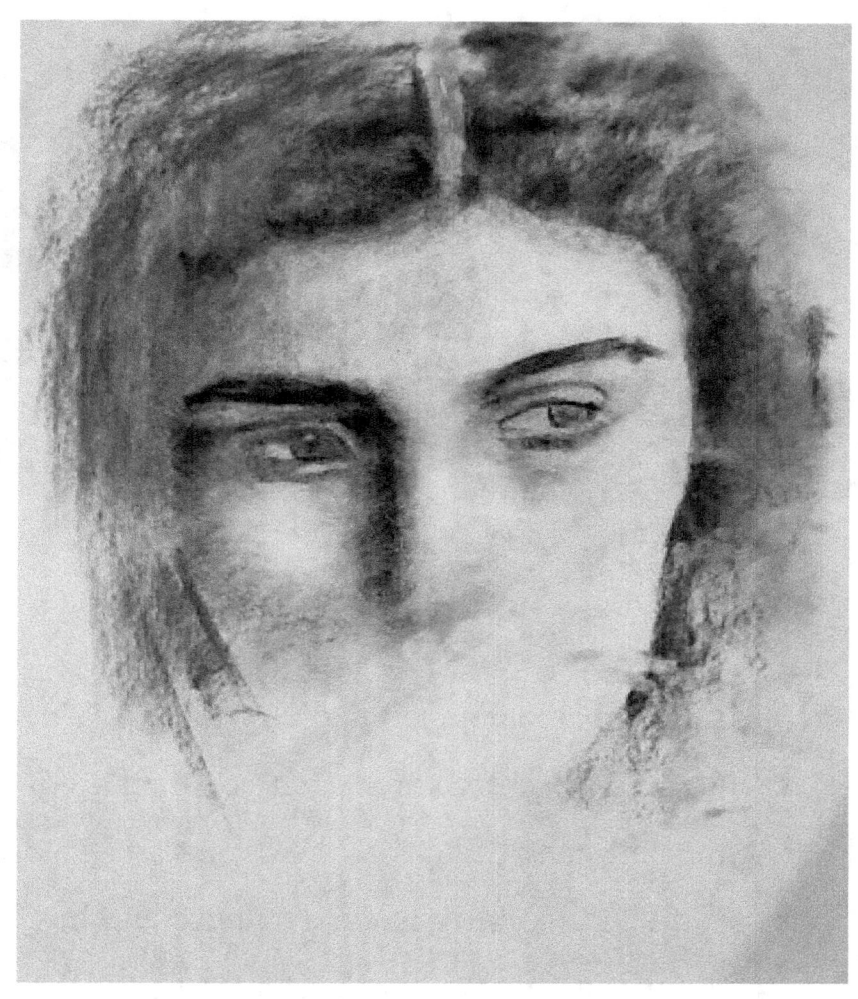

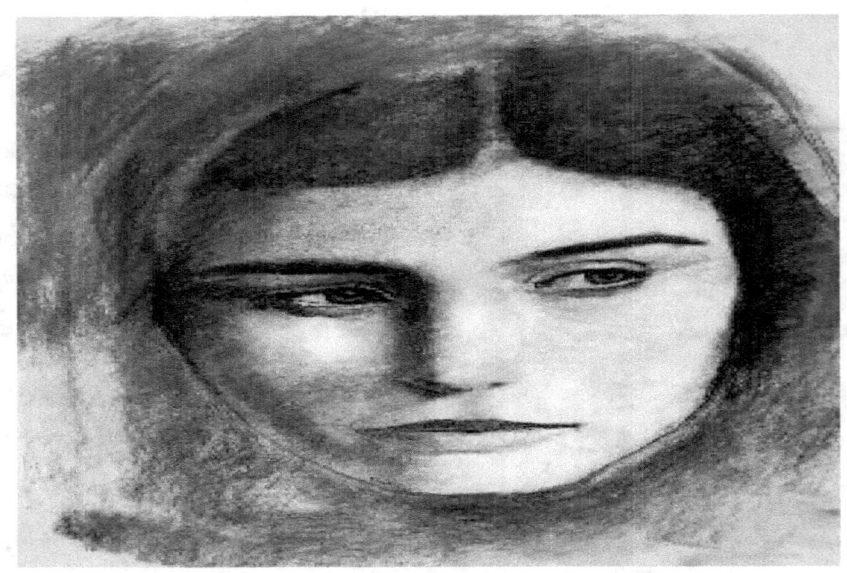

Using hard charcoal pencil to create the subtle details around the face of each area. Can you then go over it with the soft pencil to create the darker areas as well as soft brick to solidify them. The nose and lips I do last, as I try and get the eyes perfected first.

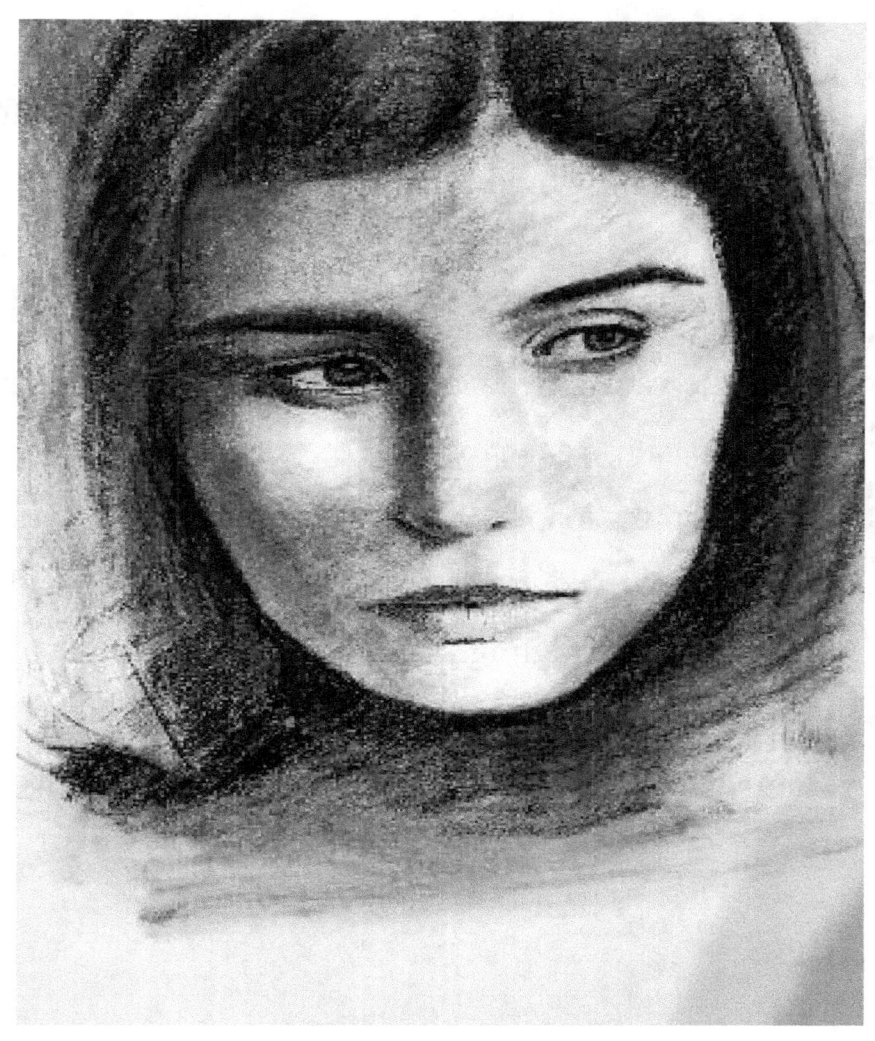

To conclude the important thing is to maintain control with using the kneaded eraser as you go through the process. A tip would be giving yourself room to use the soft pencils on the face AFTER you use the soft brick around the face etc. hair, background, shadows. Then the values will come together that way you can push the values even more on the face. To summarize; 1st cover the paper using sache, charcoal powder, vinecharcoal,2nd create shapes using stump kneaded eraser to show highlights, and 3rd comes the detailed work, using hard pencil for subtle detail, soft pencil to darken areas or soft brick to darken/solidify them.

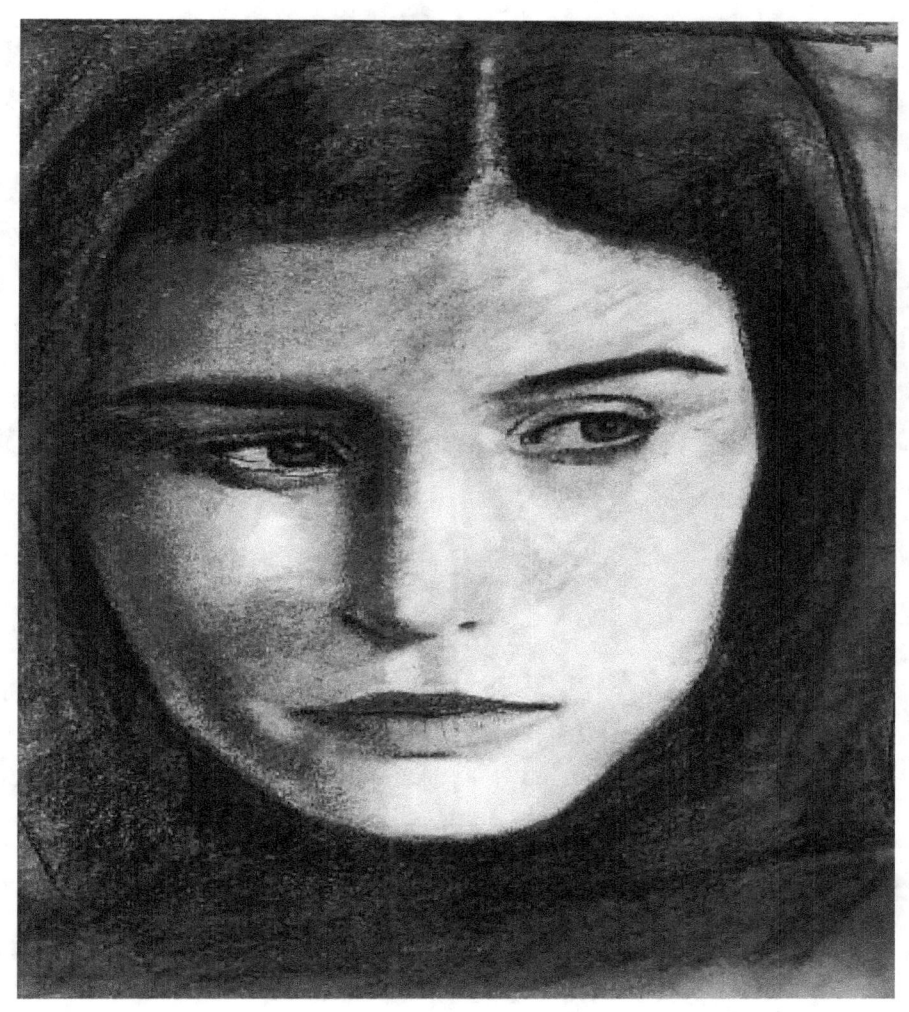

To give better examples of what's possible here are some more of my own drawings that could be used as inspiration for you to achieve after you have perfected these steps. Practice!

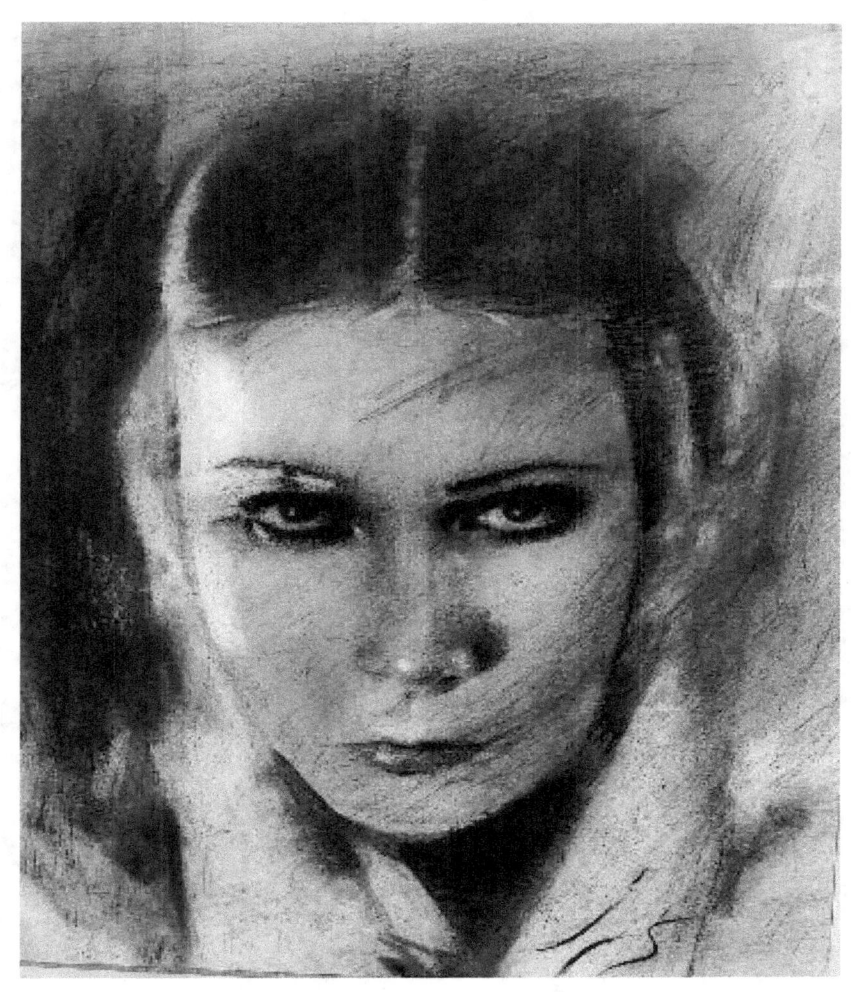

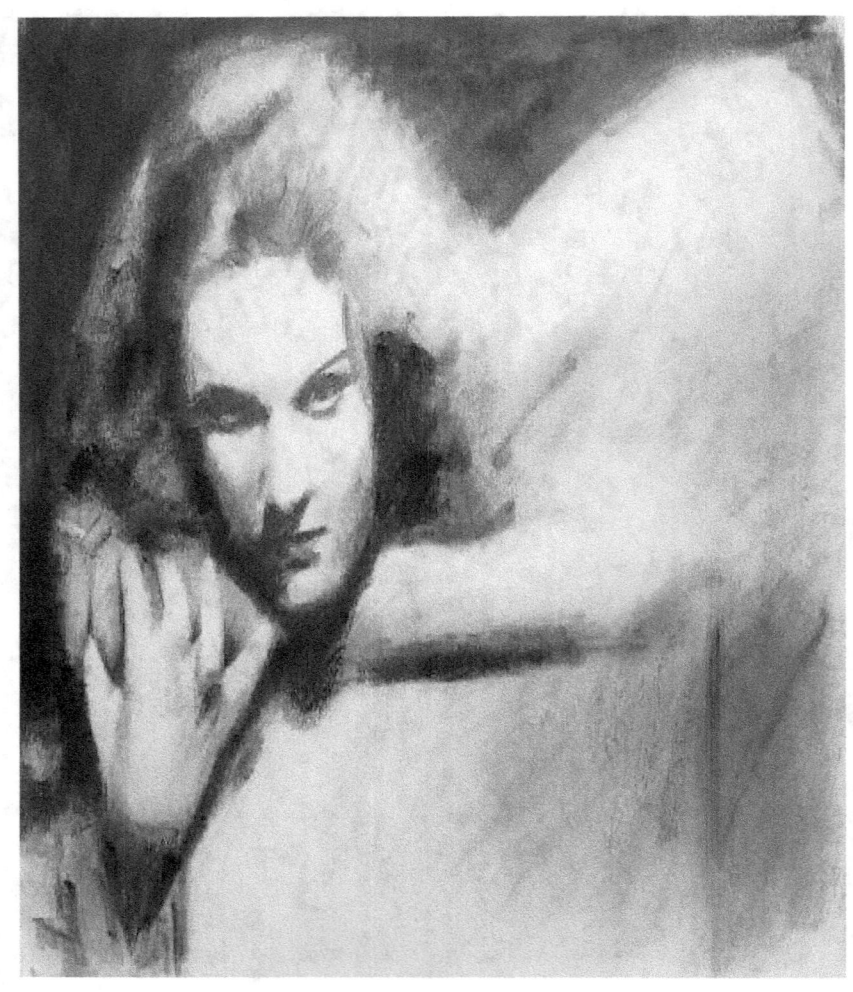

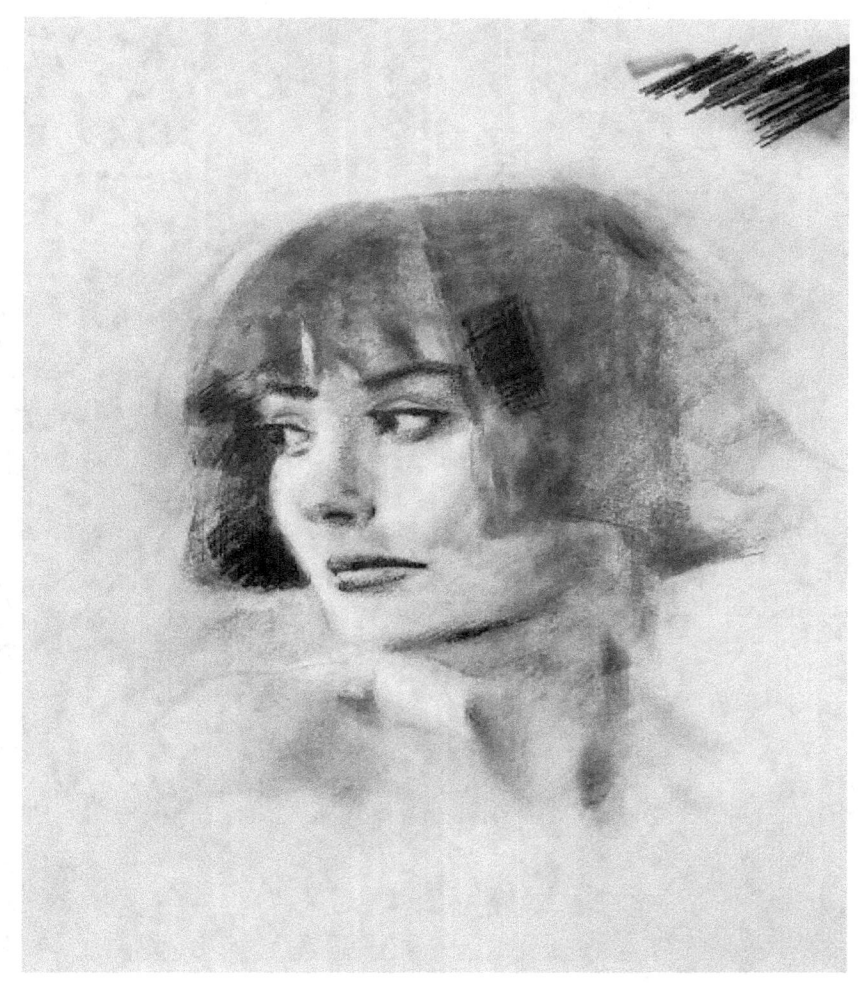

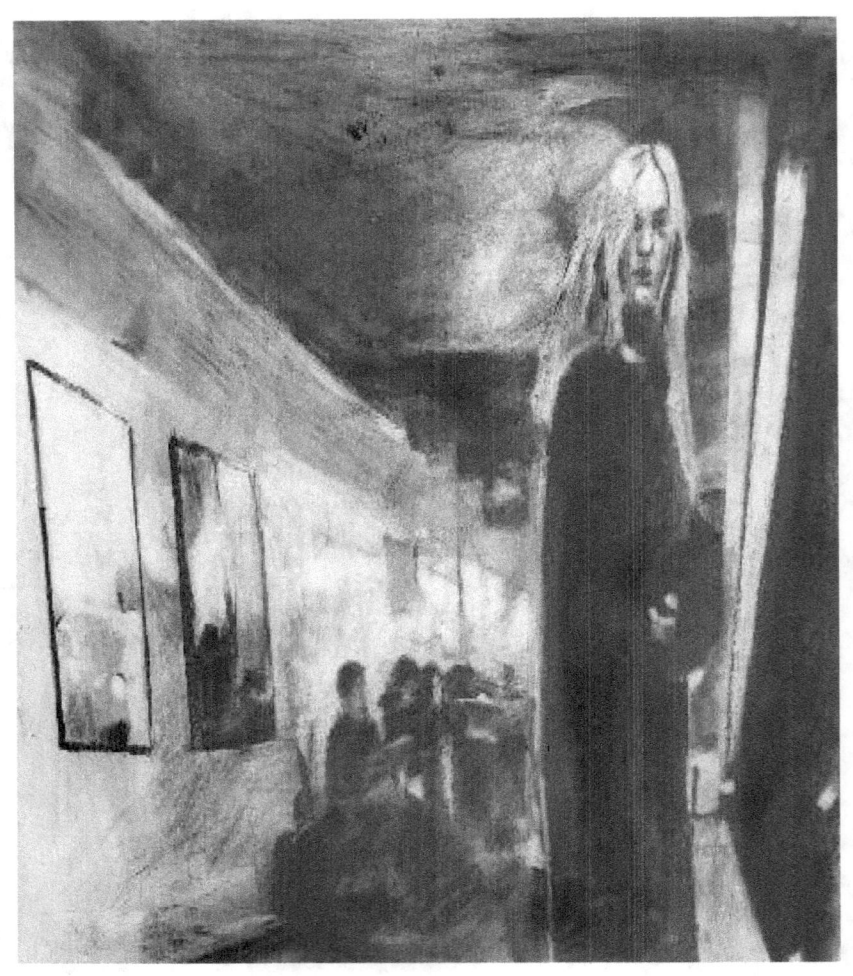

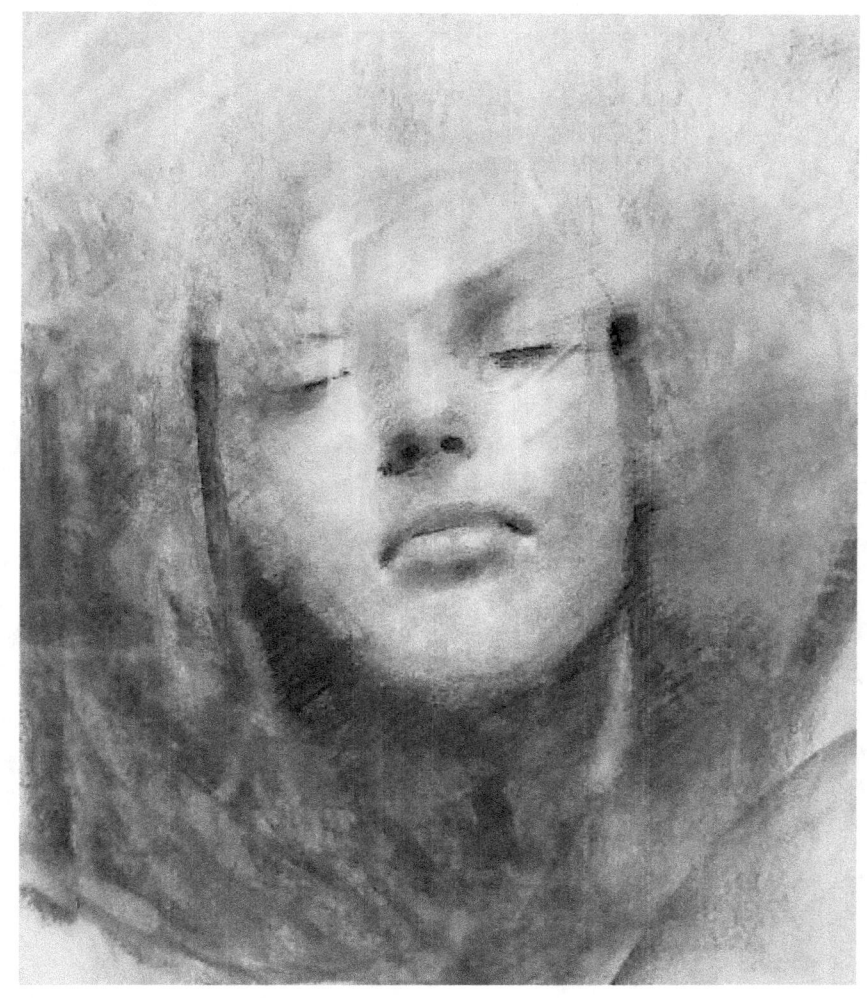

Art is the lie that enables us to realize the truth-Pablo Picasso